ANTHONY HOWELL · THE OGRE'S WIFE

D1541312

By Anthony Howell

POETRY

Inside the Castle 1969
Imruil 1970
Femina Deserta 1972
Oslo: a Tantric Ode 1975
Notions of a Mirror 1983
Why I May Never See the Walls of China 1986
Howell's Law 1990
First Time in Japan 1995
Sonnets 1999
Selected Poems 2000
Spending 2000
Dancers in Daylight 2003
Statius: Silvae (*with Bill Shepherd*) 2007

FICTION

In the Company of Others 1986
Oblivion 2002

PROSE

The Analysis of Performance Art 1999
Serbian Sturgeon 2000

AS EDITOR

Near Calvary: The Selected Poems of Nicholas Lafitte 1992

ANTHONY HOWELL
The Ogre's Wife

ANVIL PRESS POETRY

Published in 2009
by Anvil Press Poetry Ltd
Neptune House 70 Royal Hill London SE10 8RF
www.anvilpresspoetry.com

ISBN 978 0 85646 422 5

This book is published
with financial assistance from
Arts Council England

Designed and set in Monotype Bulmer by Anvil
Printed and bound in England
Printed and bound in Great Britain
by Hobbs the Printers Ltd

ACKNOWLEDGEMENTS

'How sad everything is', 'Wittgenstein' and 'Days without touching'
all appeared in *Ambit*; 'Stretch' appeared in *The London Magazine*;
'A Kingfisher', 'Sonnet' and 'Counselling' came out in *The Spectator*.
'How to End a Fairy Tale' came out in the *TLS*.

Contents

The Image

It's a photo of a girl, a photo
That he gazes at as if he were alone,
While he moves his right hand
Slowly up and down, slowly
Up and down while she watches,
Watches, from the turn in the stair.

It's a photo of a girl, a photo
Of a girl who's the image of herself,
A photo of her mother as a girl,
While he moves his right hand slowly,
And she becomes aware, from the turn
In the stair, that he is aware of being watched.

The Strawberry

The strawberry that occupies her plate
Robustly exists. Her watching it magnifies
Its bulk, which was considerable
Even before she was forced to acknowledge
Its presence as an edible affront.
How can she connive at its cessation,
Eating being a horrible sensation?
The strawberry is, well, sort of blotchy,
Rouged here, pallid there, its stubble sure
To cause internal discomfort. If she
Eats the strawberry it will become
A part of her, and, in part, she will
Become the strawberry. The strawberry
Watches her with its thousand eyes.
She has no wish to become partly
A strawberry, nor, in whole or in part,
Does she wish the strawberry to become her.
Its stalk has been removed, not its seeds,
And these she will not be able to get down,
What with her trouble swallowing.
The strawberry therefore continues to occupy
Her plate and takes over all thought.
But now it is getting ever so late,
And the strawberry has grown
Bigger than the backside of the moon.

How Sad Everything Is

Fuelled by Coca-Cola Lite,
This machine cannot have babies.
It is a work of Platonic abstraction
Subject to scrupulous maintenance
For reasons which are over-determined.

Jennifer Lopez, I love Jennifer Lopez!
She's got a big bum,
And wants an even bigger one.

Half the world hasn't got enough.
The other half toys with its dinner.
What about the children in Africa?
At least they can have children:
Got their tubes working – unlike ours.

Jennifer Lopez, I love Jennifer Lopez!

The supplement was showing off atrocities:
People got impaled in Cambodia.
How sad everything is, he said.
Some of their eyes are still moving.
People get impaled almost anywhere.

Said Jennifer . . .

Me, I got impaled, up in Cambridge.
Don't see the point now in food.
Want to wear death-camp pyjamas,
Want to have legs like a bird.
Why do what my doctor says?

Jennifer Lopez!

A Kingfisher

Frequenting a corner of an eye,
Like a thing one didn't really see,
Its dodges reconcile me
To the way you get undressed,
Affording less than a glimpse!

As for the one apparent
To our friend, eliciting
Her outburst as it darted
Close to the surface,
I guessed that stain on a backdrop

Of river and trees, that flight
I very nearly caught (but where
Was one supposed to look?)
Was lost for good. And then,
There went the streak of it

– Sooner gone than seen.
Was it, was it – what?
Sapphire? Emblem of all
Snatches: sought like the dream
One forgets even as one wakes from it.

How to End a Fairy Tale

"A girl dives into the body of a woman forever."
MILA HAUGOVÁ

A girl dives into the body of a woman forever
Or stands on the raised platform
Between trees and families spread on towels,
Her eyes closed, her lithe long legs a little bent,
Hands brought close, as in prayer.

And you can do this: tip forward and disappear
Neatly, only to re-emerge
The girl you wish so desperately to remain.
I remember someone who had trepanned himself saying
That he was now perpetually fourteen.

Repas Campagnard

Talk about boards groaning! Here prodigious
Pyramids put trestles to the test.
The horn is filled with more than it can hold.
Out roll ripe enormities; entities that split
Releasing rich excrescences. And though you won't partake,
You're led into a world where people eat
And eat and eat. Look at the broad brown thighs
On the boys and girls who bring the tureens around.
First there's the bean and beef juice soup with *lardons*
To be ladled out, but that's got butter in it,
You say, being allergic to dairy. And so you forgo
Chabrol, vintage tipped from the bowl
By those who'd wear their spoons in Breughel's caps.
They brandish bellies grander than Gargantua's,
And dance a passable *pasodoble* on their baker's
Dozen course dinners, while you sit here starving;
Your stomach being the size of a walnut now,
And the doctor worries about whether it's about to start
Eating itself, but still, on the odd wheat-beer, the *vrac*,
And the Orangina you swig, you manage to look
Slimmish, rather than skinny. It's a miracle,
And will be, till your organs all pack up.
How is it you're so juicy where you split,
With eyes that sparkle, heart-throb that you are?
As for your heart, when you die, I shall eat it;
Wash it down with good red Bergerac!

vrac: wine *en vrac* – in bulk.

Days Without Touching

The pleasure of being next to you naked is inestimable.
Where does all the time go in between?
If it goes on too long, I mean, the leaking away
Of morning followed by afternoon, and then by the rest of
    the day,
I can't get my head around anything else.
I get into a mood. Only want to think about
Crude scenarios – lose interest in galleries,
Career moves, performances, long walks in scenic spaces,
Talking on the phone with you.
Who cares what else we do,
If we can't do this; if I can't undo
What needs to be undone
And revel in the pleasure of being next to you?

Wittgenstein

I'm often anxious, as I await your coming
To see me after work. What makes me nervous
Is the fact that I can never read your thoughts.
Always, before we meet, my own desires are heated
By my ideas. I want to know you so intimately
That by the time you arrive I can hardly speak.

You step inside, take off your coat, and we speak
Of sensible, measured matters. But by coming
To see me you have betrayed how intimately
You want to be used – or have you? Truly nervous
Now, I try to disguise how wildly heated
My thoughts can get; obscene, unwanted thoughts.

Are they unwanted? How can I know? Your thoughts
May be equally wild. That of which we cannot speak
We must pass over in silence. This is a silence heated
By what we both intend to do – if I can trust your coming
Over to mean that you're not in the least bit nervous
About knowing me intensely, yes, and intimately

Too, having been here before. We both accept how intimately
Blended we can be; and when I allow my thoughts
To be voiced in the darkness later, and the nervous
Spasm of enjoyment takes you even as I speak –
Ah, it's just so perfect; to have brought about your coming
That deliciously – and to learn that you're as heated

As I am, and it seems as utterly defeated by the heated
Consequence that has transpired so intimately.
Then you turn away. Your body, moist with my coming,
Seemed to be mine, just now, although your thoughts
Have begun removing you. We hardly ever speak
After we've done it – once again too nervous

To acknowledge anything. You cool towards me, nervous
About admitting that you ever could feel heated
In the act, and that is perhaps why you speak
Of love as a thing you've never known in the least intimately,
Saying that you haven't been in love, your thoughts
Inhabit other islands, and that you don't like coming

Much – makes you nervous, I guess – although my coming
On you is ok, as is what I speak about so intimately.
As for getting heated, well – you wipe that from your thoughts.

Rosemary

Our first blue sky is laced with spring-tipped twigs,
And vigorous grasses sprout from cracks in slabs.
Her fluffy coat that shames the dwarf azaleas
Keeps her snug, this Easter Sunday, seated
On a tomb. At ease in Père Lachaise,
She eats a slice of kiwi-fruit, all leggy
In a tattered skirt: an open book
Touched by the sun that breaks on broken columns.
Then she smokes a Marlboro Light, conceding
Perpetuity to pansies mirrored in the tips
Of silver slippers, tilts a mauve beret
And taps her ash at arm's length into an urn.

Sonnet

Where am I with you? Too canny to profess
The merest leaning towards me, you may say
That words can't be relied on to express
What one feels. I sense that you delay

Making your mind up. Maybe I'm no more
Than a convenience. When Mr Right appears
Dear old Do-for-Now gets shown the door.
Sounds ominous to voice these cliché fears.

Instead, I tot up tokens of affection:
Reachings out, your chilled hand seeking mine,
A kiss on the head while working. My detection
Feeds off glances, reads into each sweet sign.

But then you say, when I put you on the spot,
"I'm just the girl you sleep with quite a lot."

The Follower

You have led me
Through long grass
To the spring
Hidden by willows:
A childhood
Haunt of yours:
Herons lift
Off its shallows.

I follow a girl
In a short dress
Underneath brambles
And onto a trunk
That grows at an incline
Out of the bank,
Prior to ascending.
Now you scramble up,

Gripping ropes of ivy,
Quite inadvertently
Showing your panties
As you raise a knee
High enough
For you to get
A toe-hold in a fork
Before you pull

The rest of your lithe
Body higher still.
Next, you're in a cock-pit,
Looking out.

I would have imagined it
A crow's nest,
But you say
That's further up.

Now it's my turn.
I peer through the gap
At my own childhood,
While you press on
Over my head,
Stretch for a branch
Way above me
And ascend from there,

Climbing beyond
My reach, your agile
Soles diminishing.
Come back, come
Down, I call,
But you won't hear
Of it, though the tree
Begins to shake,

And I cling to it,
Shaken myself,
Praying for the ground
And us back on it.
Darling, do
Come back!
I'll tread each nettle down
For you to step.

No one replies.
You have disembarked
From the crow's nest
Into the skies,
And I must get down
And go home,
But I don't think I can
On my own.

Ode to a Routine

Woken at some ungodly o'clock, you simply
Must get up; though she prefers to do it
Gradually – pushing the alarm to 'doze'
And starting off a drowsy cluck that slowly
Turns into a peck, then unassailable
Crowing minutes after it's been set.
You can't do it like that; have to arise

And go, but though the bulk of you swings clear
Some part remains attached and stretches back
To softness, warmth and slumber under the duvet.
Even so, you manage to pick up
Momentum by attending to essentials:
Teeth may well come first; then the face
Gets splashed, followed by the search for socks.

Each defers unto their own priorities.
Initially we're taught to perform these acts,
Then obliged to repeat them over and over
Till incapable – feels like progress at first.
Later each step's taken in reverse
And represents retreat: while backing out,
We genuflect, like courtiers, to our past.

That's not to say you don't long for the night
Ahead, while loading loathing on the day
Sprung on you too soon, unless brought in
A cup of tea, a juice, a slice of toast;
Or unless, once up and dressed, you make
Yourself a coffee by harsh kitchen light
That only serves to emphasise the dark

Coating the window. Put on your face or your armour
– Shaving for you, for her it's a bra and mascara –
Then run through the checklist: glasses, cap,
Key-chain, money, cards, pass, diary.
What's ahead but the heaviness of what lies
Ahead? The whole day, the whole fucking
Day of it. Hoar frost paints each turf blade

Powder white. You cross the crunchy playing
Field as orange streaks lick the night cowering
Now behind flyovers and factories.
Pressed for time, you'll take the swifter route
Past the stalls in the alley, shutters down,
Though stuff is being unloaded, left and right,
And the costermonger's occupied already;

Getting off with his underage cousin, round
By the back of the bins. The bus arrives,
The one for Seven Sisters. This you board
At the crowded fare-stage opposite Nationwide,
Or, if there's an envelope to post,
The stop up the road, past pre-arranged funerals,
Derelict pleasure-rooms, burnt-out houses of beauty.

Tottenham lurches into the day, and shoals
Of Pakistani school-kids share the aisle
With Roma in Romany dress, Lithuanians,
Workmen with power-drills, priests, mothers up early,
Keen to be first in the queue at the surgery
Or that immigration place. A dark
Smile rolls marbles at some pert remark

On a mobile. High browns hit high fives on blacks.
Hair comes curled in wet-look slicks
Or corn-rowed on cranial plantations.
African London overwhelms these decks:
Suited, or gaudily costumed, redolent
Of cocoa-butter, sandal-wood and musk.
Breathe in as you squeeze past patterned rumps.

Breathe out when alighting next to Tesco's.
Hurried past, the supermarket glows,
Promoting an untimely aura of spruce
Organisation: nearly every till
Attended, all the shelves restocked: the bright
Fluorescents left on every single night
Adding a lustre to the hardening daylight.

Who's a shopper, though, at ten-to-seven?
Bent on earning, curse the lit-up gent
Who stops you while inviting swarms of cars
To hurtle past, until they brake at last
And fingers drum on steering wheels or pick
At noses. Tunes get set and ciggies lit
While time drives on, leaving behind a dam:

Taxis, bikes, commercials and articulated
Tankers; old crocks; luxury jeeps
And other affluent influx from forested Epping;
Alfa Romeos on order to footballers' wives,
And sleek limousines picking up rap artists early
To get to a Nottingham gig – all obliged
To idle as the infantry go by:

Teachers, nurses, plumbers, tea-boys, chefs,
Cleaning ladies, secretaries, clerks,
Management consultants, sales girls, geeks:
Duplicates of those at the other end
Of the city hurrying across the lights:
Their aim's to get wherever you are already.
This is the downside of being in one body

At a single time, though might it not cause
Cancer – being beamed from place to place?
Once upon a time a moving staircase
Proved a source of wonder: rows of lines
Gliding flattened out of metal combs
And turning into steps – the stupid bitch!
Hasn't she learnt to stand on the right? What

Do they teach them, back in Lithuania?
Clutching *The Times* you made a detour for,
Down you thunder, two steps at a time,
Into the intestines of metropolis.
You place yourself exactly on the ledge,
Wary of contact, keeping, as far as you can,
Apart, which could be yards or could be inches.

If you're lucky, something's on its way.
The rails begin to snicker to themselves
About its coming – if you're not, you wait,
Perhaps for aeons. How many deadly hours
Are spent fuming on platforms like ravines
We can't bridge for ourselves? In queues, at counters,
Holding receivers, shifting on our pins,

We fume, until we pass through pearly portals.
Doors arrive and open now. You're off,
Contented, with a seat for once secured;
Although your sedentary movement, well,
It's nothing but another sort of waiting.
Here we go, in our millions, getting where
We want to get to maybe, maybe not.

Packed in together, never deliberately touching,
Nodding to the iPod, hardly there,
Leafing through the tabloid to some hot spot
Harbouring disaster or desire,
Unless the angle's right to catch a person
Reapplying. As the lips compress,
Daydream on a scheme for her address.

No need to change though. That at least's a relief.
No stampeded steps or gradient passages,
Or girl ahead, who reaches round to tug
Her top down at the back, to read your mind.
This line will take you straight through to Vauxhall,
Passing under roadworks and foundations,
Polishers and hoovers and those nipper things

They use to tidy street and shopping mall.
Purposed or purposeless, you are a merry corpuscle
Jostled in the stream where everything
Is plural – you contribute to the plasma
Circulating through this urban hydra;
Moving along in a grimly juddering silence,
Blasted by a tumult you ignore.

Try to hang on to your inner space, to pray
That you won't get stuck a thousand feet below
Trafalgar Square or Bank or Pimlico.
That's what a person under a train can do.
And they deserve to die in the nastiest way
For the claustrophobic torture of delay
They've wished upon a myriad commuters.

Ground to a halt, in a tunnel, forgotten about.
Certainly no excuse for being impunctual!
Thank God Vauxhall comes sliding into view.
You get off here, to glide up from the bowels,
Oyster an eye and activate the barrier.
Time to buy a roll: its spicy lamb
Gets micro-waved and then you're on your way.

Sneaking past the home of MI6,
Festooned with hearing aids that listen in
To dirty thoughts as well as dirty tricks,
You mount the stairs that lead up to the overland.
A nip here, in the air, unlike the fetid air
You've come from, and a platform crowded
By incoming travellers appropriating marches:

Doing what you're doing in reverse
– Avoiding the *melée* of Waterloo.
A train drifts in. You choose a window seat,
And now tracks veer away from your trajectory.
Bridges flit by overhead and ads
Unreel along the route and serpentine
Expresses pass with an ephemeral hastiness:

Aimed at the centre, as you travel out,
Passing London's power-station folly,
Streets of roofs, rows of backs, the park;
Town halls, tower-blocks, tops of double-deckers:
Multiples repeated every day;
Multiples compounded by the times
You've seen them pass below these moving panes,

Come rain, come shine, in daylight, in the dark.
At length you reach a duplicate of Clapham
Junction that's a pretty good impression,
Given it's today, of yesterday.
Out you get, descend into a tunnel,
Battle human waves to reach the gate,
Thread the dense arcade and hit the street.

Past Moss Bros, dodge behind a bus to cross
The road and round a corner to your stop.
Now for the worst of all waits, while running short
Of seconds to squander. See how the minutes go down
On a screen inside the shelter outside Debenhams
That once was Alders. Here the juggernaut
Delivering Shoefayre's trainers blocks a lane.

Buses again, pulled up, queuing both ways
To inch past a wing-mirror continentally sized,
Only to get obstructed by some nut
Pulling out from behind the lorry's back.
Stupid bloody bastard! Fucking prick!
These exchanges lead to no reverse:
The jam gets worse, as does the language, but

The passengers can only watch and wait,
Everyone convinced that they'll be late.
Their journey, though, is shorn of any content:
Boredom, rage, revulsion – just a maze
Of vacant forms, and isolated movement
Robbed of all identity by number.
One becomes a cypher, nothing more.

There's no more you. There's one. There's a statistic
Waiting to be counted. That is all.
Eventually one's bus arrives. The driver
Lets the ones on board off first. The ones
Who're waiting then pile in. The doors behave,
And the bus moves at a snail's pace up the rise
Observed by blackbirds perched on someone's grave.

And then, beyond the graveyard and the school,
In an outer borough far removed from one's own,
One's out of the bus and hurrying up a lane,
Then, at a gate-house, proffering an ID,
And the door slides shut behind one. Once inside,
One cuts across a sterile outer yard,
Opens the wicket, closes it of course,

Locks it, proves the lock, and does the same
With the next lock and the next, until one's deep
Inside a place which others can't get out of,
Can't enjoy the freedom one enjoys:
That liberty to travel, to commute
From one place to another, heading back
After one has served one's daily sentence.

Blessed Are the Weeds

Neither man's nor woman's, hardly land;
Ground perhaps; but ground devoid of places:
Slivers of soil, providing a toehold for brambles,
Thorny patches, wedges without purpose,
As between some confluence of lines
Sheared off by a wall between two bridges.

Each lacuna's denizens do well:
All those unreachable copses beyond the pale
Asylums for intransigent varieties;
Specimens whose fibre has no worth.
Nobody seeks to bed *them* – their seeds
Aren't on the roster of the park authorities.

Where jettisoned though, these develop roots
As tough as any ragwort's, grasp the nettle
Cussedly, to thrive in wiry multitudes
For all the dearth of nitrogen in such
Unhallowed spots. Blessed are the weeds
For they shall inherit the earth.

Childhood

I am trying to reanimate the spell of it,
Most poignantly the feeling that it would last forever,
That we could go on stowing away
In the bellies of horses towed into Troy.

Then mayhem would topple the nettles,
And wouldn't we make our escape
By following dachshunds through hedges
Into another adventure, fugitives from "The End"?

Back then, there were places whose existence
The giants never acknowledged:
Thickets where we would peel each other's wands.
Other children . . . They were other lands.

Between release and re-arrest for tea,
God knows what we got up to.
Weekends packed us into the loft
As close as sardines. We held our breath.

The giants came and went, or paused,
And you could get eaten, of course,
If you didn't do what they said, or perhaps
You just got eaten anyway. You see,

There were caves: if not Ali Baba's,
The scout-master's den, the vestry
Where we went along with it occasionally.
These were the giants' own hideaways

Where they betrayed the fact that they were children
Even more deliciously forbidden
Than we were forbidden to ourselves:
But weren't their knees a joy to climb?

Everything comes back; how one settled oneself
Knowingly in the saddle, working away
At their innocence – always a guise –
With fingers worse than waves

When the tide is on the rise.
Back in those days, the girls would tuck
Their skirts into their knickers when they sailed
Over the horse in P.T. Their teacher

Dreamt of their tummies. They knew it.
We knew it, being unruly by nature,
As we all were, in that other Narnia
Where Aslan mated with Lucy.

Parable

No one had given it much thought before.
Supposedly it went on, as everything must, somewhere,
Occupying its place in the mazy tarantella
Of existence where every variation, aberration
From the norm, executes its insignificant party piece.
Evolution depends on it, one could argue,
Since change is often brought about by freaks.
Some of these may be throw-backs: others
Improve on the model, fitter than their origins
To carry on. But even so, this untoward phenomenon
Appeared to be as rare as any minor element;
A trace, no more, and difficult to get wind of –
On the whole surviving as a mere figment of literature,
Outré, to say the least, if it went on at all,
That is, until it was mooted, mostly for the sake
Of consistency, that it should be an article of policy
To stamp it out altogether. Oddly enough,
No sooner had it become prohibited than it began
To crop up, at first only in rumours or backwaters,
But these faint indications would suffice
To bring about some tightening of the legislation.
After that, it proved a mite pernicious:
The law had become quite scrupulous in its aim,
Which is to say a wrong had been defined,
And it was clear that a quite considerable number
Sensed that it now fell to them to rise to its occasion.
People, the very same people who had hardly
Given the business a thought, suddenly discovered
In themselves a propensity to perpetrate
A freshly heinous misdeed. The outrage it provoked
Helped them to enhance their identity, it seemed:
Each felt less like some particle of carbohydrate,
More like an element, vital, if quite rare,

Albeit no longer obscure, notorious, rather.
Penalties increased, and more than a few chose
Serially to commit this ever more serious crime.
Again, the law was improved. And today,
Entrenched, draconian, its aim is to nail down niceties,
Closing the loopholes flagged up by acquittal.
That is why we are queuing here to be sentenced,
Or wreaking on you all an excess of illegality
In this growth area generating horror and employment.

Nature Reserve

Willows kiss the lock's black timbers.
Moor-hens nod upstream. I down
My cider and head off into the marshes.
Herons lope over lines. Cow-parsley
Tall enough to walk beneath is rampant here,
And beyond the blackberries screening
A cement plant, past the reservoir
Sealed off behind a marina, water-meadows
Isolated by causeways for the overland
Stretch towards the river's alder thickets.
This is where the grass grows high
And I remove my clothes – to fold them
Neatly at my feet. Naked, now, I stand
So that the sun may toast my back
And so that my buttocks may be shown
To those who are surely watching from the train.
Barley tickles my thighs. I pose
With arms akimbo, exposing my front
To couples filching nosegays from
The footpath's fringes. Cormorants neck it
Past alders. I am erect as a heron
And having a scarecrow effect
On lovers heading for the toppled willows
Reached through a urinated underpass
To my right. These willows make for labyrinths
In the air, enclosed by leaf-lit canopies,
Where slender women hang as fruit
In the moonlight, ripening, night after night,
For the rapist waiting behind the water-filtering unit.
He may have his way beneath the burrs,
But I have no prey. I warn off passers-by.
And, as the sun goes down, I put my clothes back on
And amble home, stoned on my recollections.

Crusted Portcullis

The castle was infested by rats,
Its crenellations askew, its masonry
A hazard. Here were drains hampered
By gauntlets, dungeons knee-deep
In gore, and a pitch-stained atmosphere
Prevailing. Sadly crippled cats
Were mocked at by the rodents
For getting kicked to pieces by the soldiery.
Water-logged, a barge lay sunk
In the moat where a bellwether floated,
Bloated, sodden, motionless.
A thin hand brushed the cobwebs
Free of bats, and the lady
With the rope hair-do lisped awhile
Of bygone feats and feasts that were not woebegone.
Once her barge had glided, water-tight,
If oft befogged by dew and exhalations.
Later, though, her lusts were made redundant,
Meek, lascivious sin banned to the wild wild north.
She made to moan, but brightened:
"I'll not long remain. Truth to tell,
I yearn to view those bergs that ride the deep,
And there are no rats in Iceland."

Bacon

Here he is sweeping the children
Up into entirely fresh flutterings
Of uncaged conversations as
He enters yesterday, throwing open
Its grey doors and allowing the
Breeze to shiver reflections in
The mirror at ease with the blossom.
Some of them have gone shopping
In the woods for cones where
Honey drips into the puddles of
A calm evening. Yes, although a
Scratching from behind the wall
Continues unremitting in the penumbra
Of this afternoon, and one gaunt thorn
Spoils the dappled path where a
Lovely creature in a suave girdle
Tells her desires to the birches.
Surely she deserves better than to
Slip up in the suburbs, pocketing
Some ready cash for the drudgery
Of nuzzling in the back of his car?
Gnarled work bringing on the spasm
Of his gaunt reek, her head in
His murderous creases. What would
He have her – a whimpering cur
In the detritus of her writhing? Dregs
He downs when grassed on by his
Bleak and contaminated cronies.
Never more will he ponder this in the
Garden, with nothing to the seasons now
But temperature, the grate of gates,
Verrucas, and the sour stench of age.

Bacon: prison slang for a sex offender.

Where You Begin to Believe

These tables have been designed to prevent
Us getting our legs underneath them:
If they were lower, as in the Orient,
Maybe our class would sit on its knees
To look at the bars. Any three of these
Might be the foot of the sign for *Shan*,
Though not its cloud-wreathed peaks.
Still, from the uppermost floors, the fours,
You can get a glimpse, they say,
Of the very tips of some distant trees.
One of the finest things to contemplate
Is the white board, after it's been cleared
Of grammar and the simplest of sums.
A sea of mist, it might be, seen
From a height. So perhaps my cell-mate
And I are lounging in some easy pine
Meditating on a waterfall. A path
On stilts has been allowed to pick
Its way across the falls further down.
Those on parole are taking the ledge road
Up, up, and again up, above
The floating islands into the floating mountains.
We are erasable markers, wiped away
By the mist which teaches us
That the pines could turn into demons.

Counselling

My advice is this: if you must assault a person,
Offer them a hand up afterwards. Others don't.
And if you will add rape to the assault,
Never indulge on a regular basis.

If you have to rape a person once or twice a week,
See if you can stop yourself from killing them.
Should you feel compelled to rape and kill,
Try at least to steer clear of children.

If you really need to rape and murder children,
Do it in a nice way, perhaps while they're asleep;
Though if you're set on eating one alive,
Why not choose the least attractive specimen?

Oh, I'm aware that it's hard. It's the attractive ones
That whet the appetite. Still, there's always worse,
It's good to reassure oneself. Take genocide:
A decent person does it by surprise.

Stretch

Three years it's been now since I felt the rain.
We get to shower every now and then.
For storms I'll have to wait as long again.

There is our daily amble round the yard,
But if it's raining – whether soft or hard –
We're banged up by some hydrophobic guard.

When clouds deface a postage stamp of stars,
And drizzle dulls the hum of distant cars,
Try catching drops by reaching through the bars.

To get well soaked would suit me to the ground:
To stand there as the rain fell all around:
To piss in it and revel in the sound.

Tell you one thing, when I'm on the out,
With underwater hands, I'll tickle trout
And sleep rough till I've made up for this drought.

Inmate

I'm walking towards antelope
In the bush. Look how they spring
To their feet and leap off
Into the distance.

The Ogre's Wife

A call for visitors was posted in the church gazette.
Prison seemed my cup of tea. I hunted sinners well
And truly worth it, not the undistinguished sort I'd met

Mired in mere adultery. Did any merit Hell,
As I did, I was pretty sure, for one polluted thought
I'd hesitated to confess? I craved the authentic smell

Of misdemeanour, which is how my pious nature caught
The attention of my Destiny. As I was paying heed
To someone else, one came and sat. The other quickly sought

An exit. Left alone with sin incarnate, I agreed
To struggle for his soul. It felt as if he'd come for me –
A monster others whispered of. His appalling creed

Was soon to give me anxious nights. Because I sensed he saw me
As some catch he'd finish off, that thought of mine took hold:
A prideful notion – that a fiend was destined to adore me,

Making Heaven glad as he was led back to the fold.
Ah, but the assailant proved at least as strong as God!
His gaze was chilling, yes, and yet, it hadn't left me cold,

Although it spoke of irises left bare beneath the sod.
I saw those eyes as you might see them just before you died.
A precipice accompanied the narrow path I trod.

Then a friend went to Japan and sent me a card of a terrified
Woman clamped by her sex to the snout of a giant octopus:
Pleasured, or disgusted? One was hard put to decide.

At our next encounter, a mistral began to brew in us.
Then he touched – it felt as if my clothing blew away
Together with my sanity. It all seemed too ridiculous

For words. I watched a film that night, about a fish that lay
In wait for males or females, darting out to copulate
Or kill. It was the same with him. I might end up his prey.

I might become his mate. It wasn't clear to him what fate
Was mine. He simply went for me, began to haunt my sleep.
I thought he'd kill me. Wanted out. But it was now too late,

And I deserved to be destroyed, for coveting this deep
Liaison with a source of darkness. Then they let him out.
He'd got my number off me while I'd still had hopes I'd reap

The benefits of winning him for Jesus. More devout
Than sensible, I'd prayed to save his soul as if my life
Depended on it. Did such ardour put my faith in doubt

And our Redeemer test it then by making me the wife?
If so, He handed me the role I'd dreamt of in a drama
Set on earth to mirror Hell. That gaze cut like a knife

On meeting in a bleak café – little of the charmer
About this one. I was disembowelled there and then. The joy
Would come, I knew, when every last impediment of armour

Fell away, and, naked, I was his: a chattel to employ
Exactly as he willed. So be it. Here stood his lamb for the slaughter.
But I was too eager. I bore him first a girl and then a boy.

Hostages? Accomplices. He needed son and daughter,
Never threatened. Still, I felt it foolish to oppose him.
He might then reject the bed, forsake the conjugal quarter

Of his life, its one consoling refuge. So to swim
Against his current wasn't right. Nirvana, if release
From pent-up urgency, gets enhanced by fear, however slim

The chances are that you can circumvent the need for peace
That moves your executioner. After we'd had intercourse,
I'd lie there, panic on the ebb – would contact the police,

If I could get away, that is. I never did, of course;
Hugely humbled, grateful that he'd chosen not to stop
My breath on this occasion. Church would never bless divorce

From duty allotted, namely to stay the devastating crop
Of murders if I could. Although I failed, and failed again,
My forgiveness mattered. He was just the one on top

Of the situation, just as the will of powerful men
Crucified our Saviour. Me, I lay in ecstasy
Beneath him. Psychiatrists may learnedly insist that when

I went with him initially some suicidal part of me
Came to the fore – acknowledged – though I did not wish for
    death
As such. To risk it as I rose to pleasure: agony

Perfected – as it might please Mary, when she received that
    shibboleth,
For the angel to appear in his inordinate splendour,
Glory ablaze, to experience the empyrean breath

And be consumed by Word made Fire from which no shield could
    defend her
Any more than my presence could protect the girls he came
Across on his hunting trips, my hubby, for whom there was no
    surrender

That was acceptable, other than mine, no offering the shame
Of meek desire as your Pekinese will, set on by a mastiff,
Nor need anyone declare that I should bear much blame.

I was a decent girl, after all, albeit rather passive
While at the convent where you were either principled or damned.
Some of the girls there opted for damnation in that oppressive

Atmosphere at variance with the times. Having had it rammed
Into them that sex was wrong, they took a flippant view
Of immaculate conception, and were sure the sisters shammed

Their abstinence. They masturbated, everybody knew!
Wine was good for nothing else but to get pissed, party and shag on.
Not in the least like them, I really thought that it was true

That sex was wrong. I was not prepared to jump aboard the wagon
Of their promiscuity. Lust was a covert activity
Hardly even sanctified by marriage – devised by a dragon

Or worse. How could you accommodate both piety
And arousal, or justify an appetite for the soiled
Hungers of the lower body? Cleanliness and Chastity,

These were the Cardinal Virtues, whereas having sex embroiled
You in a cauldron no one ever clambered from unscathed –
To perish in the bestial act, though, left the soul unsoiled,

By way of being a sort of retribution – you were saved,
Or at least your soul was. So, for me, to hazard being deprived
Of life made sex conceivable. I had this engraved

As well: my risking death in wedlock actually revived
My partner's chances of remission. Thus did the Lord ordain
That I should serve. The sinner might be saved if I survived.

None of his crimes weighed much compared to what God
    stood to gain
Through me. Victory over Satan would be absolute
When at last we brought this being, penitent, to cleanse the
    stain

On his conscience. When he went hunting, I would choose
    the route,
Sat in the van beside him. He would roll his window down
Since he declared that he could scent the ripe yet unplucked
    fruit

As if he were a unicorn. He joked about the renown
Of this beast, and how it pierced the zone that it identified
Even as it sought the unsullied lap, but then he'd frown,

For he wasn't always correct, nor did he ever once decide
To abandon his plan if the girl had been with a beau or had a
    bun
In her oven. He acted on impulse, just like the fish, however
    he tried

To justify his choices. Certainly the Infernal One
Prompted him as much as I was moved by the Righteous Being.
Then it was *my* job to lower a window, always with our son

Or daughter sitting on my knee, clearly installed for the seeing,
Offer the lift from which the girl at the verge would never alight.
Into the back of the van she'd climb – and there was no fleeing

For her after that from what was an inevitable fight
Between good and evil, between my spirit and his: a desperate
Engagement this, rendering her contribution trite.

He took her home occasionally, and I must needs commiserate
With the creature, "Make your peace, my dear. The chosen are
    but few."
I meant it: these were the ones he chose to rape and lacerate

At leisure. Others, alas, he took by force without ado
Then strangled on the floor of what he called his chariot
Of desire. I used to watch in the mirror. The view

Gave me a way to assess her worth. Did she tarry at
The stake, or did she embrace it greedily? And did she
Seek my glance in the glass? Oh, I was worse than Iscariot,

In her estimation, I guessed; but if she succumbed too easily
Then I'd report to our Lord that she was not for Paradise.
Purgatory for her then, at the very least. For me,

Whatever her response, once he'd gone inside her thighs
She deserved the rest – intact no longer, had she ever been –
Just a slut who humped with him before my very eyes.

Why did I let it happen, though? I still relive each scene,
Reflecting on my inertia, as I watched in that mirror, appalled.
Perhaps because normality would right itself between

One killing and the next. We lived at peace. And if I'm called
Abettor, then I claim this mitigating victory:
When it happened, Love prevailed, and Lucifer was mauled.

My husband dug their graves beforehand on our property.
He tipped them in, he covered them, stamped the turf down
    tight,
Then, to receive my blessing, afterwards he'd come to me.

Yes, and I knew everything, yet still survived the night.
This was a miracle. Was he not Mortality made flesh?
And since God died as Jesus, he'd killed God, he'd killed the
    light!

Ah, but in the double bed, where, bloodied, we'd enmesh,
I was Death's entire salvation, by God's Grace appointed
Gleaner of this abject portion else left behind in the thresh

Of spirits winnowed at the Trumpet, when the world's anointed
Rise on the Day of Judgement, making all creation whole.
. . . Yesterday, though, an inspector called and it was pointed

Out to me that certain secrets land you up in gaol.
Recently too I have gathered that the wife of a neighbouring
    ogre
Just got thirty years for not being able to control

His appetite. My outlook's altered, since I took up yoga.